Explore new ideas!

Welcome to your Reading/Writing Workshop

Read exciting literature, science and social studies texts!

Become an expert writer!

Build vocabulary and knowledge to unlock the Wonders of reading!

Use your student login to explore your interactive Reading/Writing Workshop, practice close reading, and more.

Go Digital! www.connected.mcgraw-hill.com

Cover and Title pages: Nathan Love

www.mheonline.com/readingwonders

Copyright © 2017 McGraw-Hill Education

Send all inquiries to:
McGraw-Hill Education
2 Penn Plaza
New York, NY 10121

ISBN: 978-0-07-677063-2
MHID: 0-07-677063-X

Printed in the United States of America.

7 8 9 LWI 20 19 18   C

Program Authors

Diane August	Jan Hasbrouck
Donald R. Bear	Margaret Kilgo
Janice A. Dole	Jay McTighe
Jana Echevarria	Scott G. Paris
Douglas Fisher	Timothy Shanahan
David Francis	Josefina V. Tinajero
Vicki Gibson	

Mc Graw Hill Education

Unit 1

Getting to Know Us

The Big Idea
What makes you special?.... 6

(t) Guy Francis; (b) Jason Chapman

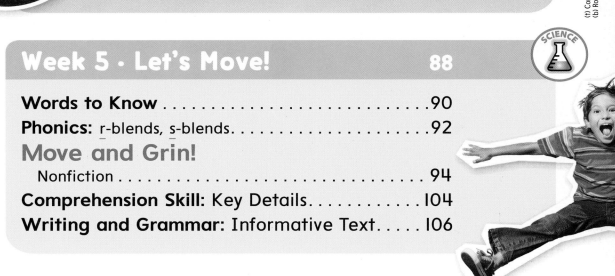

Unit 1

Getting to Know Us

Something About Me

There's something about me

That I'm knowing.

There's something about me

That isn't showing.

I'm growing!

The Big Idea

What makes you special?

Essential Question

What do you do at your school?

Go Digital!

Back to School

Talk About It

What are these girls doing in school?

does

Dan **does** his best work.

not

Do **not** run at school.

school

We read a lot in **school**.

what

What can we play today?

Your Turn

COLLABORATE

Say the sentence for each word.
Then make up another sentence.

Go Digital! *Use the online visual glossary*

11

Short <u>a</u>

The letter <u>a</u> can make the short a sound in **p<u>a</u>ck**.

<u>a</u>x   c<u>a</u>n   s<u>a</u>d

f<u>a</u>n   h<u>a</u>t   j<u>a</u>m

p<u>a</u>n   r<u>a</u>n   m<u>a</u>p

t<u>a</u>ck   b<u>a</u>ck   w<u>a</u>g

Nan ran back to the mat.

Nan sat on the mat.

Your Turn

Look for these words with short a in "Jack Can."

Jack   can   Max

sad   Nan

Guy Francis

Genre Realistic Fiction

Essential Question

What do you do at your school?

Read about what friends can do at school.

Go Digital!

Guy Francis

14

Jack Can

Max can.

Can Jack? Jack can.

Max can. Can Jack?

Jack can **not**.

Jack is sad.

What does Nan do?

Nan helps Jack!

Jack likes **school**.

Key Details

Key details help you understand a story.

Words and pictures in a story give you the key details.

🔍 Find Text Evidence

Find key details about what Jack can do.

page 17

Can Jack? Jack can.

Detail		Detail		Detail
Jack can make a picture of himself.	⇒	Jack can not reach.	⇒	Nan helps Jack reach.

Your Turn

Talk about key details in "Jack Can."

Go Digital! Use the interactive graphic organizer

25

Write About the Text

Jack Can

Pages 14–23

Matt

I answered the question: **Which activity seems most challenging for Jack? How does this change?**

Student Model: *Informative Text*

Jack can not write a word.

Jack can not reach up.

I see that Jack is too short.

Clues

I used evidence from the story's words and pictures.

This makes Jack sad.

Nan gets a stool for Jack.

Now Jack can reach.

Focus on an Event

I wrote about when Jack got help.

Your Turn COLLABORATE

How do Jack's feelings about school change? Use text evidence to support your answer.

Go Digital!
Write your response online.
Use your editing checklist.

Essential Question

What is it like where you live?

Go Digital!

Outside My Window

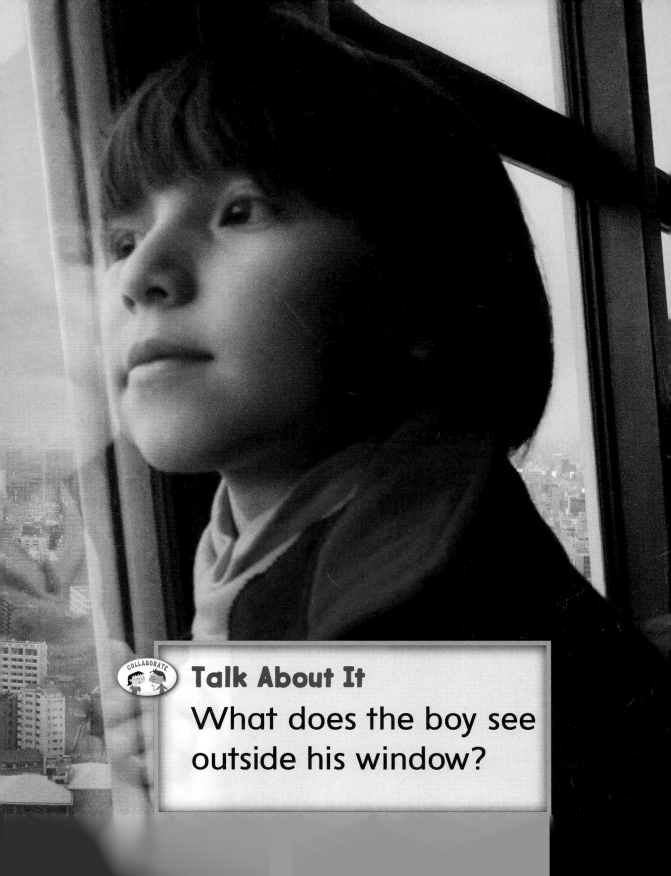

Talk About It

What does the boy see outside his window?

down

We go **down** the steps.

out

They go **out** to play.

up

They went **up** the hill.

very

It is **very** loud in the city.

COLLABORATE

Your Turn

Say the sentence for each word. Then make up another sentence.

Go Digital! *Use the online visual glossary*

31

Short i

The letter i can make the short i sound in **six**.

it	is	sit
him	big	dip
kid	pig	lid
sick	kiss	miss

Nick ran up a big hill.

Will he sit with Jill?

COLLABORATE

Your Turn

Look for these words with short i in "Six Kids."

six   kids   hill   dig

pick   dip   will   fix   it

Genre Fantasy

Essential Question

What is it like where you live?

Read about what an animal family does where they live.

Go Digital!

34

Six Kids

Six kids go **out**.

Jason Chapman

Six kids go **up** a hill.

Six kids dig, dig, dig.

Jason Chapman

Six kids go **down**.

Six kids pick, pick, pick.

Six kids are **very** blue.

Six kids dip, dip, dip.

That will fix it.

Six kids like it here!

Key Details

Key details help you understand a story.

The sequence is the order in which the key details happen.

🔍 Find Text Evidence

Find a key detail about what the six kids do first.

page 37

Six kids go **up** a hill.

44

Detail	Detail	Detail
First six chicks walk up a hill carrying farm tools.	Then they dig holes to plant seeds in their garden.	Then the six chicks pick blueberries.

Your Turn

COLLABORATE

What happens next? Talk about other key details in "Six Kids."

Go Digital! Use the interactive graphic organizer

Write About the Text

Pages 34–43

Sasha

I responded to the prompt: **Describe where the six kids live.**

Student Model: *Narrative Text*

The six kids live on a farm.

The farm is on a big hill.

The grass is green.

Details
I used details to describe the farm.

Grammar

The **words** are in the correct **order**. The sentence makes sense.

46

There are lots of berries.
The farm is near a pond.

I figured out more about the farm from the picture on page 40.

Your Turn

Describe how where the six kids live affects what they do. Use text evidence to support your answer.

Go Digital!
Write your response online.
Use your editing checklist.

47

Essential Question

What makes a pet special?

Go Digital!

Special Friends

COLLABORATE Talk About It

What pet do you have or would you like to have?

be

A turtle can **be** a fun pet.

come

My bunny will **come** to eat.

good

A cat is a **good** pet.

pull

I **pull** my dog in a wagon.

COLLABORATE

Your Turn

Say the sentence for each word. Then make up another sentence.

Go Digital! Use the online visual glossary

l-blends

The letters bl, cl, fl, gl, pl, and sl make the beginning sounds in **black**, **click**, **flat**, **glad**, **plan**, and **slim**.

flap	slips	flag
glass	blip	clap
class	flips	blab
plans	slick	slam

Our <u>c</u>lass pet is named <u>Sl</u>ick.

<u>Sl</u>ick can <u>fl</u>ip in its <u>gl</u>ass bowl!

Your Turn

Look for these words with l-blends in
"A Pig for Cliff."

<u>Cl</u>iff   <u>gl</u>ad   <u>Sl</u>im

<u>bl</u>ack   <u>sl</u>am   <u>sl</u>ip

Essential Question

What makes a pet special?
Read about Cliff's new pet.

Go Digital!

Constanza Basaluzzo

54

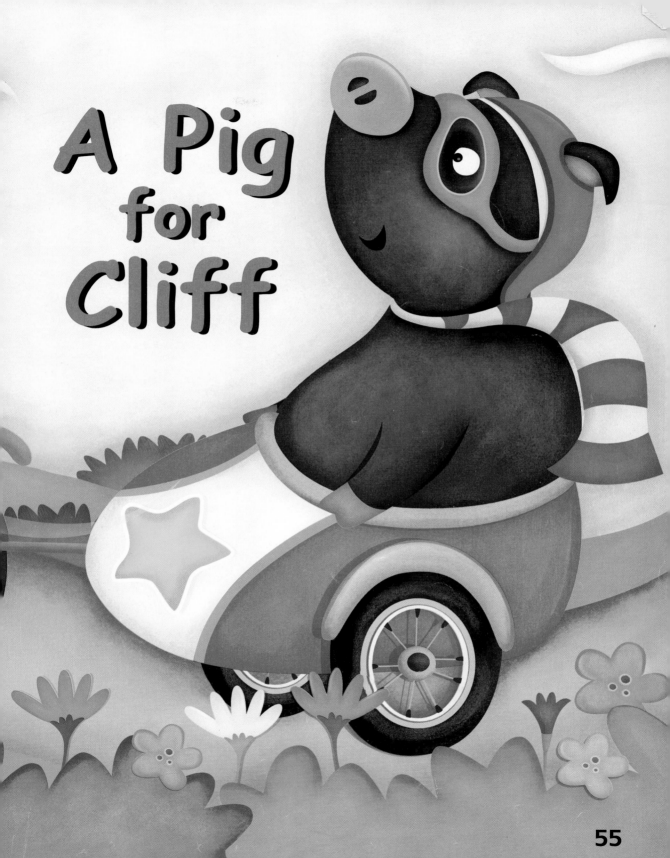

A Pig for Cliff

Cliff is glad.

Cliff has a new pet.

It is Slim.

It is a big black pig.

Slim can not fit in!

Come out, Slim!

Slam!

Cliff can not sit with Slim.

Cliff and Slim slip.

Slim can go up.

Cliff can not.

Slim can **pull** Cliff.

Slim will **be** a **good** pet!

Key Details

Key details help you understand a story.

Key details happen in order, or in sequence.

 Find Text Evidence

Find a key detail in the story.

page 57

It is Slim.

It is a big black pig.

Detail		Detail		Detail
Cliff has a big, black pet pig named Slim.	→	Slim breaks the swing, so Cliff and Slim fall in the mud.	→	Slim pulls Cliff up out of the mud. Slim is a good pet.

COLLABORATE

Your Turn

Talk about your favorite details in "A Pig for Cliff." Tell about them in order.

Go Digital! Use the interactive graphic organizer

Write About the Text

Pages 54–63

Marco

I responded to the prompt: **Write a new story in which Cliff brings home a different pet.**

Student Model: *Narrative Text*

Cliff has a new pet dog, Max.

Max loves to tap dance!

Cliff does not tap dance.

Cliff gets on his bike.

Characters

I created a make-believe character. I told what he likes.

Describing Details

I told what the character does.

Hola Images/Getty Images

66

Grammar

A sentence that tells something and ends with a period is a **statement**.

Cliff comes back.

He has new tap shoes.

Max and Cliff dance all day!

Your Turn

 COLLABORATE

Write a new story for Cliff and Slim. How do they get into trouble? How do they get out of it?

Go Digital!
Write your response online.
Use your editing checklist.

Weekly Concept Let's Be Friends

Essential Question

What do friends do together?

Go Digital!

Just for Fun

Talk About It

What do you and your friends do together?

fun

It is **fun** to play tag with friends.

make

We can **make** funny hats.

they

Can **they** go up and down fast?

too

We like to skate, **too**!

Your Turn

COLLABORATE

Say the sentence for each word. Then make up another sentence.

Go Digital! *Use the online visual glossary*

Short o

The letter o can make the short o sound in **hop**.

box	top	rocks
not	lot	fox
jog	clock	toss
dolls	hot	mops

Can Ron jog on a hot day?

Ron can jog a lot!

Your Turn

COLLABORATE

Look for these words with short o in "Toss! Kick! Hop!"

toss   hop   block

dolls   flop

Genre Nonfiction

Essential Question

What do friends do together?

Read about how friends play together.

Go Digital!

74

Toss!
Kick!
Hop!

Kids play together.

Kids zip, zip, zip.

Kids toss, toss, toss.

Kids kick, kick, kick, **too**!

Kids **make** block houses.

Kids make dolls.

Kids hop in sacks.

Hop, hop, flop!

They have **fun**!

Key Details

Key **details** tell important information about the selection.

You can use photos to learn key details.

 Find Text Evidence

Find a key detail that tells about one way that friends play together. Use the words and pictures.

page 78

Kids toss, toss, toss.

Corbis Bridge/Alamy

84

Detail		Detail		Detail
Kids toss balls.	→	Kids make dolls.	→	Kids hop in sacks.

Your Turn

COLLABORATE

Talk about other key details in "Toss! Kick! Hop!"

Go Digital! Use the interactive graphic organizer

Write About the Text

Pages 74–83

Penny

I responded to the prompt: **Write a new title for the selection. Tell how it is different from the original.**

Student Model: *Informative Text*

My title is "Fun With Friends."

The old title is about moves.

The kids do more than move.

The kids play together.

Compare and Contrast
I told how I made my title different.

Clues

They make houses and dolls.

The kids smile and laugh too.

They have fun with friends!

Grammar

An **exclamation** shows strong feelings and ends with an exclamation mark.

COLLABORATE

Your Turn

Look at the different things that the children are doing to have fun. How are they the same? How are they different? Use text evidence to support your answer.

Go Digital!
Write your response online.
Use your editing checklist.

JGI/Jamie Grill/Alamy Stock Photo

Essential Question

How does your body move?

Go Digital!

Ready, Set, Move!

Talk About It

How are these kids using their bodies?

jump

Do you like to **jump**?

move

It is fun to **move** to music.

run

My dog can **run** fast.

two

The **two** cats like to play.

Your Turn

COLLABORATE

Say the sentence for each word.
Then make up another sentence.

Go Digital! *Use the online visual glossary*

r-blends, s-blends

The letters br, cr, dr, fr, gr, pr, tr, sk, sm, sn, sp, st, and sw make the beginning sounds in **brick**, **crab**, **drip**, **frog**, **grass**, **prop**, **trap**, **skin**, **smack**, **sniff**, **spot**, **still**, and **swam**.

brag	**crib**	**drop**
grab	**swims**	**track**
skips	**snaps**	**stop**
trip	**stick**	**spill**

Fran can run, spin, and skip.

Gram stops to see Fran's trick.

Your Turn

COLLABORATE

Look for these words with r-blends and s-blends in "Move and Grin!"

grin	frog	Scott
swim	Fran	trot
Stan	crab	grab	Skip

Essential Question

How does your body move?

Read about how animals and kids move.

Go Digital!

94

Move and Grin!

Paul van Hoof/ANP Photo/age fotostock

Scott's frog can hop and **jump**.

It can **move** its back legs.

Scott can hop and jump, too.

Hop, hop, jump.

Fran's dog can swim a lot.

It kicks its **two** front legs.

Fran can swim a lot, too.

Swim, swim, swim.

Stan's horse can trot and **run**.

It jogs on its big long legs.

Stan can trot and run, too.

Trot, trot, run.

Skip's crab can grab.

It can grab with its claw.

Grab, grab, grab.

hand

head

arm

leg

foot

Skip can grab, too.

Grab, grab, grab.

What can Skip grab with?

103

Key Details

Key details tell important information about the selection.

You can use words and photos to learn key details.

 Find Text Evidence

Find key details that tell how Fran's dog moves. Use the words and pictures.

page 98

Fran's dog can swim a lot.

It kicks its **two** front legs.

First Light/Alamy

Detail		Detail
Fran's dog can swim.	→	It kicks its two front legs.

Your Turn

Talk about the key details in "Move and Grin!"

Go Digital! **Use the interactive graphic organizer**

Kevin Zimmer

105

Write About the Text

Move and Grin!

Pages 94–103

Rose

I answered the question: **What steps does Skip take to reach up high? Use first, next, then, and last.**

Student Model: *Informative Text*

This is how Skip reaches.

First, Skip looks up.

Next, Skip lifts his arm.

Clues

I used the photo to answer the question.

Order of Events

I told things that Skip does in the **order** he does them.

Then, Skip raises his foot.
Last, he grabs with his hand.

Grammar

This sentence is a **statement** telling what Skip does.

Your Turn

COLLABORATE

Use <u>first</u>, <u>next</u>, <u>then</u>, and <u>last</u> to describe the steps needed to make Fran's motions. Use text evidence to support your answer.

Go Digital!
Write your response online.
Use your editing checklist.

Rubberball/Mark Anderson/Getty Images